Small Talk for Introverts

How to Start Conversations and Make Friends Managing Social Anxiety and Shyness

Larry Newman

Table of Contents

Introduction

The following chapters will discuss what you need to know as an introvert, or someone who is shy, about starting small talk. As an introvert, you probably would rather spend your time at home, reading a book, watching a show, or doing another hobby that might not be considered "social". This is how you recharge your batteries and get a break from all the socialization that you get at work or at school.

But there are just some situations where you need to talk to other people, and the small talk that ensues can be difficult, and often brings you to a screeching halt with nothing to say.

This guidebook is going to help you deal with social conversations, and can make you an expert at small talk, no matter what your experience level was before. If you are a shy introvert, being able to hold a conversation and turn that simple small talk about unimportant topics into a deeper conversation later on is so important, and will help you to make the lasting friendships that you need and desire.

In this guidebook, we will look at a few different topics, especially about how introverts and shy people are two different personality traits (you can be shy without being an introvert, and not all introverts are shy), and how they view the world differently.

From there, we are going to explore valuable tips that will empower you to become great at small talk. We will look at how to become an active listener, rather than just thinking about what you will say next, how to be more likeable, and more.

There are so many instances in our lives when small talk can be important. And for a shy introvert, these times can prove to be a challenge. Most introverts would rather just stay home and not do too much socially. But they may still need to show up to events for family and friends, for work, or to make some new friendships. This guidebook will provide the tools needed to really get some great results with small talk, while still celebrating all the things that make an introvert unique!

What is Small Talk?

Before we explore some tips that will help you improve your small talk skills, we first need to understand what small talk is. Small talk is a type of socially acceptable conversation that is essentially meaningless when it comes to its content, but it can serve an important function in certain situations and contexts.

For example, in many English-speaking countries, it is seen as unfriendly or rude for people not to participate in small talk. When you are looking for the right subjects to talk about with this kind of polite conversation, it is expected that you will stick with non-personal comments over non-controversial subjects.

Small talk is a way to be pleasant, for a few friends to catch up quickly, or just to pass the time when you are waiting for an event or in line, it is not the time to get into all of your political views or try to get a debate going. Keeping the conversation as light and breezy as possible is the key to ensuring that the small talk goes well.

A good example of small talk is discussing the weather. In fact, this is one topic that many of us already use on a daily basis when we run into people that we see only occasionally, or when we meet someone new. For example, you may find that as you chat with the cashier when getting your groceries that you talk about the weather, or a bit about your plans for the weekend.

Making conversation like this can sometimes be related to the situation at hand, such as waiting in a line. How many times have you been waiting in line at the store or at the post office and then started talking to someone nearby about how slowly the line is moving that day? You may use small talk and other forms of communication with those you see each day, but who you don't know very well. Another good example is a person that you run into in the halls of your apartment, but never really talk to for more than a few minutes.

Small talk can also be common at parties, such as when the guests all know the host, but they don't really know each other that well. During this time, it would be considered rude, and a little bit awkward, if no one mingled or talked to each other. So, each person will start getting together and talking about inconsequential subjects to help break the ice.

One way that this can be done—especially at a party—is with a compliment, such as one woman complimenting another on her dress. While compliments are acceptable, they also shouldn't make the other person uncomfortable, by referring to the person's body or sounding like a pick-up line. Guests who are at the buffet table could talk about the food that is offered, as they decide what to put on their plates to eat.

The point here is that small talk is not supposed to be very in depth. Since most small talk occurs between you and someone you don't know at all, or at least someone you don't know very well, you really don't want it to get much deeper than how long the line is taking or the weather recently. Keeping things light and airy is the point of small talk. The more general you can keep the topic, the better it is for everyone involved.

There are some people who love to use small talk. They may like to communicate in a verbal way with other people, or they may find the silence uncomfortable in some instances. There are others who like to meet new people and find that they really enjoy talking and learning more about them. Some people don't like this small talk at all, and often dread going out or going to a party because of it.

Every person deals with small talk differently. Some people find that they can meet up with anyone and form a connection with each person they come across. And then there are those who really struggle with small talk and maybe carry around a list of topics with them so that they can think of things when the conversation tends to lag a bit.

For many introverts, engaging in small talk is a challenge. They may already have a hard time talking to other people, especially those they don't know well. Perhaps they are already struggling with the venue or the situation they are in if it happens to be loud, new, or something that they don't particularly enjoy doing.

There are also some social constraints that happen with small talk, which can make it difficult to know what to say, putting further pressure on introverts who struggle with being out and around other people. Add to this that many introverts are shy, and small talk can be a pain. Just because someone is an introvert and needs quiet time alone, without being around people all the time, doesn't mean that they don't like people at all. They just need to take a different approach.

This guidebook will help with this. With some practice, and some time, even the shyest introvert will get better and they will see success. Anyone can learn how to use small talk to their advantage, they simply need to be ready to take some time to learn how to do it!

Based on the majority of the research that has been done on the topic, most people are happier, and experience a greater sense of well-being, when they are around other people. Being alone and in isolation for more than short amounts of time, even if you tend to prefer this, can be hard on the health. People who engage in conversations that are more meaningful, rather than just small talk, have a greater sense of wellbeing as well. But how do we build up to those deeper conversations? We need to start with small talk.

You usually don't end up in a deep and meaningful conversation with someone you just met. Instead, you start out with some basic small talk, and then, over time, you build up to the deeper conversations, the ones that are so good for your health.

If you are an introvert, or shy, or emotionally sensitive, small talk can be difficult, as this kind of conversation seems pointless and empty of meaning. However, it is unlikely that you can meet someone new, or even start a conversation with a friend, by just diving right in to any big issues that you have.

Always remember that for the most part, small talk is just the beginning of your connection with other people. It is going to be hard, and there will be times when you aren't going to want to do it. Maybe it feels the same as having to go out and get groceries and clean the house before you can have company over that you enjoy spending time with. The preparation is going to take work, and it is not going to be much fun. But once you have the company over and enjoy yourself, all that work seems worthwhile.

This is also true for meeting people and engaging in small talk. It is hard to do, and sometimes it doesn't always go the way that you would like. But after you have made a new friendship or a new connection with another person, you will find that the small talk was all worth it. You will feel good that you went out to a social event and made an effort.

When you work to build up your social skills with small talk, you will find that it becomes much easier to reach the deeper conversations and relationships that you desire.

Almost everyone runs into some trouble when they are working with small talk, and only a few people are naturally good at it. But if we want to be able to form deeper connections, friendships, and relationships that are so important to our wellbeing, we need to start somewhere, and that somewhere is with small talk. This guidebook is going to provide you with a lot of tips and tricks that you can use to get better at small talk, and to help you see the best results possible in no time.

Clever Ways to Start Small Talks

Now that you're aware of some potential topics to talk about, it's time to know exactly how you can pull it off and initiate the conversation. Note that even if you're knowledgeable about possible topics for small talks, you will still have a hard time pulling it off if you don't know exactly how to deliver it. This chapter will cover some of the most useful tips that can help you during this stage.

Ask open-ended questions

A lot of people prefer to talk about themselves, so tapping into this is a great way to initiate small talks then keep the conversation going. Open questions require explanations, instead of just a yes or a no response. They often start with what, who, how, where, why and when. Closed questions, on the other hand, begin with are/am/is, have, and do. An example of open question are what type of music do you love the most and why? This often requires an explanation, so you can do away with a simple yes or no as an answer. Since there's an explanation, you can respond and lengthen the conversation.

Refer to previous discussions

If you will be talking with someone whom you've already talked to before, then it would be best to have a mental list of topics that you talked about before. You can then continue talking about one. Some examples would be a bad news he shared to you, a project he's working on, or a recent achievement of his child. Aside from giving you an idea about what to talk about, it can also make the other party feel better, since this shows that you are actually paying attention to what he's saying. It shows him how good of a listener you are and that you care about the experiences and problems he shared with you. This can further encourage him to build a connection.

Ask questions that he can easily answer

To successfully initiate small talks, and ensure that the conversation will keep going, you need to make sure that you ask questions that the other party will never have a hard time answering or responding to. Keep in mind that there are certain questions that are extremely difficult to answer. If you want to engage someone, raise easy and interesting questions that he will definitely love to answer. This can help ensure that the conversation will flow even better and more smoothly, making the two of you feel more comfortable.

Be sensitive

You can't just bombard someone with questions without considering about whether he's willing to talk about the topic/s you're interested in. If you're asking him a question, make sure it's non-invasive. It should not be related to topics they don't want to discuss. For instance, there are those who may feel irritated or distressed if you ask them about issues that affect them personally. These include weight, inadequate qualifications or skills, relationship issues, etc. Be sensitive and thoughtful. Avoid talking about issues that will invade their privacy or make them feel bad about themselves.

Say the name of the person you're talking to from time to time

Aside from helping you remember his name, it's also a good way to show your respect and to make him feel comfortable. Referring to him using his name can make the conversation even more personal, intimate and real. This will establish more connection, so don't be surprised if you notice that the small talk you initiated actually turned into a smarter, deeper and more meaningful one.

Stay engaged

Make sure that you don't make yourself look bored when talking to someone. Make him feel like you are really engaged in the talk you've initiated and that you're interested about what he's saying. Show him how willing you are to keep the discussion going. Focus on him, as well. Ensure that your curiosity remains piqued, instead of trying to withdraw back to yourself. This tip is crucial if you want to retain a more comfortable and light conversation and make sure that it continues.

The good thing about keeping yourself engaged during the entire duration of talking to someone is that it will give you ideas about the topics to talk about in your future small talks and conversations. This is especially true if you're going to talk to the same person again. This will instantly give you a hint about what you could possibly discuss about, such as asking for an update about a certain aspect in his life.

Be natural

When initiating small talks, you don't have to force yourself to act like someone you're not as this can only make you feel too uncomfortable. Be natural. Respond to situations based on how you normally do. Laugh and smile naturally each time someone makes a joke or funny remark. Avoid forcing laughter, though, as this may alarm him. Smile and nod naturally. Be yourself and you will most likely bring out these reactions naturally, instead of making them look forced and awkward.

Don't worry too much about pauses

There's nothing to worry in case there are some pauses after you've talked about a certain topic. The good thing about pauses is that you can actually use them to change topics. These also serve as a way to take a short break or breather and re-energize the small talk. There's nothing to worry about unless the pause and silence is already too long. Avoid stressing yourself because as long as you excuse yourself for a while, or move naturally into the next subject, then you're all good.

Don't be afraid to get a little more personal

This is a useful tip, provided you determine first if the other party is willing to talk about something personal. One advantage of getting more personal, with the consent of the other person, is that you get the chance to get closer to him more quickly. You can easily become more familiar about him, making it easier to build a connection. Some safe topics, despite being a bit personal, that you can talk to him about could be his favorite book, his favorite sports team, his passion and hobbies, and his favorite holiday.

Ask follow-up questions

Once you've initiated a small talk, be sure to pay attention to his responses. This is a huge help in weaving good follow-up questions. Your follow-up questions will also keep the conversation going. Just make sure that you don't probe too much to avoid annoying him. Your questions should still be answerable by something, which he finds comfortable in.

Avoid making your small talk partner uncomfortable, as well. Be sensitive on his responses – be it verbal or non-verbal. It's also advisable to be more respectful in your response to someone who stays uncomfortable or awkward with you around. If the person you're talking to seems uninterested to share details or info or seems withdrawn, then avoid persisting too much.

While asking follow-up questions is essential in keeping the talk going, learn when to stop. Avoid asking too many questions if he starts to become unresponsive.

Chapter 1

Introvert and Extroverts

Despite what a lot of people may think, being introverted and being shy are not the same. They may have a lot of similar characteristics, and on the surface, they can look the same, but they do have some big differences. An introvert enjoys spending their time alone, and they can sometimes feel drained emotionally if they spend a lot of time out with others. But a shy person doesn't enjoy being alone, they are just afraid to interact with those around them.

What is the difference

Let's consider two children who are in the same classroom. One of these children is shy and the other one is an introvert. When the teacher organizes an activity for all of the children in the class, the introverted child might prefer to stay at their desk and read a book because they find that spending time with the other children in the class can be stressful. But the shy child would really like to join in with the others, but they stay at their desk because they are scared to go over and join them.

Introversion is an intrinsic part of a child's personality and you won't be able to change or force them to act against their nature. But children who are shy can be helped to overcome this shyness. There are some introverts who are also shy, but this isn't true of all the introverts you meet. In fact, some of these introverts have excellent social skills, they simply choose not to interact all of the time because this leads them to feel drained, and they need to spend some time alone so that they can recharge their own emotional batteries.

While it is possible to use different techniques and even some therapy to help a person who is shy to overcome this obstacle, trying to turn an introvert into someone who is outgoing, or into an extrovert, will cause them a lot of stress and could make their self-esteem drop. Introverts are able to learn some different coping strategies that will make it easier for them to deal with a variety of social situations, but no matter what, they will always be an introvert.

Those who are dealing with shyness have a hard time when it comes to meeting and talking to someone new, and they don't like to find themselves in a brand-new situation. They might even feel so much fear about being in these situations, that they have physical symptoms, like blushing, shaking, sweating, and heart palpitations. It can sometimes be severe enough that it can cripple the individual and impact on their mental and physical health.

Of course, everyone can be shy in different types of environments, and there are a lot of different degrees when it comes to shyness. Most people are shy without having it turn into a problem and they will be able to use techniques to get over it.

Shyness and introversion are two personality traits that are often written down as the same thing by those who don't have to deal with both, one, or the other. Outgoing extroverts find it hard to see a big difference between these two personality types, and they just assume that all people who are shy are introverts, and all introverts are shy. But this is not the case. It is possible for these two personality types to exist inside one person, but it is not a guarantee.

We have all been to one of those parties. There is that one person that is standing to the side, or maybe they are still within the group, but they look like they do not want to be there at all and are just waiting for the best chance to leave. In some cases, if you are an introvert, you are that person. Many people don't take the time to learn about these two personality types and how they differ, and they will brush it off, and this can get really grating on the individual, who feels like they are misunderstood.

One study that was done by the Salk Institute for Biological Sciences suggests that there is actually a different way that the introverted brain registers the world around them compared to others. When researchers took the time to study the activity in the brain of someone who is an introvert, it was found that the same amount of electrical activity occurred when they looked at an inanimate object and when they looked at another person.

This could really suggest another reason why a lot of introverts just don't want to look for social interaction. They not only get tired from doing it and feel a bit drained in the process, they may also find that this social interaction isn't stimulating to them at all, so they don't want to waste their time with it.

The introvert will go out on occasion. It isn't like they will never talk to others or that they avoid talking at all costs, and they do have friends as well. But they know their limits, and they know when they would rather be at home doing something else. And since introversion is more of a biological personality trait, most of those who are dealing with it are going to be completely fine heading home at the end of the day to be alone or spending their break time reading a book, instead of interacting.

While an introvert would choose to stay home on a Friday night because they don't see the interaction as stimulating, or they need to recharge their batteries after a long week, a person who is dealing with severe shyness may think that their only choice is to stay home, even though they wish that they could be out and about instead.

There are also some extreme cases where those who suffer from this kind of shyness will find that they can't function in many situations. For example, they may find that they can't ask for something as simple as directions from a stranger. Or, they may find that they aren't able to go to the front of a check-out line because then they will need to interact with another person.

Introverts are good at finding small groups of friends. When they have some people that they are close to, they can be great listeners, and they will provide thoughtful advice and be empathetic. But a person who is shy may find that it is more difficult to form the close friendships that they need. They may even feel awkward around people, including family and those that they have known all of their lives.

Introverts who are not also very shy can be fine if someone comes up to them and begins a new conversation out of the blue, even if the long conversation leaves them tired. But someone who is shy may find the thought of starting a new conversation—especially if they need to initiate it—terrifying.

The main difference between these two traits is how the person feels about the lack of social interaction and companionship. An introvert is fine with this. Even though others will assume that they aren't okay and will try to convince them to go out, the introvert is usually happy with the results that they have. But for someone who is dealing with shyness, they tend to wish that they could go out and have more friends. They are the ones that feel there is something holding them back and they just aren't able to put themselves into the situations that would make this possible.

You may have never been called an introvert in the past. Maybe you have done a really good job of hiding your personal feelings and inclinations. Maybe you aren't an introvert and really are just shy.

Before you get too caught up in this whole introvert climate, you need to know what an introvert truly is.

The most accepted definition of introvert is: a quiet person who does not find it easy to talk to other people.

An introvert isn't a people person. The introvert is more comfortable hanging back and sticking with people who are familiar. It isn't exactly accurate to say an introvert isn't comfortable talking to other people because talking to their best friends and very close co-workers is going to be very easy. In fact, **the introvert may just be the life of the party when it is people who are close and familiar**.

It is also defined as someone who focuses on oneself. That makes it sound like an introvert is self-centered in a bad way. That is generally not the case at all. An introvert isn't stuck-up or self-centered but, because the introvert chooses to avoid others or mind their own business, they often get labeled as such.

People who see the introvert standing back and only talking to a select few people may be dubbed aloof because they are not mingling or making the social rounds.

An introvert isn't going to be the person that walks into a party and starts introducing themselves and chatting with complete strangers.

The introvert will likely migrate to small groups of people with at least one familiar face. An introvert is probably not going to be the life of the party in this type of situation and will prefer to only talk to the few people he or she knows. This is **why they tend to earn the label of being stuck-up**.

An introvert is also labeled as antisocial. This is a tricky one because, in reality, an introvert is antisocial by the true definition, but not against all people in general.

It is just the fact they prefer their own company. An introvert will be emotionally drained after spending any length of time in social situations that require them to talk with others. It is nothing personal; it is just the way an introvert is wired.

<u>Are YOU an Introvert?</u>

Now you are probably a little confused. Are you really an introvert? Are you shy, but actually an extrovert? Oh, labels are so much fun—not!

In this case, a label is okay, because it is going to help you maximize your strengths. You can wear your introvert or extrovert label with pride and not be ashamed of who you are.

Everyone has strengths and everyone has weaknesses. Being one or the other doesn't make you better. It doesn't mean you are more worthy of a promotion at work and it doesn't mean you are ineligible because of your base personality traits.

This small checklist will help you determine whether or not you are truly an introvert or maybe you are just a little shy or anxious about being in public. **Answer each question honestly.**

There isn't a wrong answer. Fudging the truth is only going to make it more difficult for you to tap into your strengths.

- You prefer to be alone over spending time in large groups. A Saturday night at home on the couch or doing your favorite hobby is far more appealing than hanging out at the club or going out with friends. You enjoy your solitude and would rather turn on some music at home alone and just chill;

- Being in very public, social setting is physically and emotionally draining. It may only be a couple hours, but by the time you get home you will feel as if you have run a marathon or been up for days. It depletes your energy completely;

- You don't always want to talk on the phone or even respond to texts. When the phone rings, you may ignore it or send it to voicemail more often than not. It may take several minutes or longer for you to text back a friend. The sheer act of conversing while you are in your zone takes a lot of strength that you may not always have;

- Small talk is draining. An introvert prefers conversations about things that are actually relevant and important rather then mundane conversations that will be forgotten 5 minutes after they are done;

- You notice things about your surroundings and people. An introvert is naturally more observant. By not talking and socializing, you have more time to take in your environment;

- When in groups, you are usually quiet and doing more listening than talking. You only talk when you have something of value to add to the conversation;

- You tend to think before you speak. You are not one to fly off the handle, and you will take several seconds or even longer to respond to a question;

- You are probably a bit standoffish and are not willing to accept anyone at face value. An introvert needs to evaluate each person and determine whether or not they are honest and who they really say they are. You are slow to trust;

- You don't find yourself truly bored very often. An introvert's mind is always busy thinking about various situations and planning. Mulling over past and current problems is a common way to pass the time. You may find you like to read, do puzzles and other activities that allow you that quiet, deep introspect that recharges you;

- Your best friend has been your best friend for a long time. When you make friends, they are lifelong commitments. You rarely allow anyone into your inner circle. Rather than having a large group of friends, you only have a close few that you enjoy spending time with;

- You are probably the go-to person when your close friends need advice. Your ability to analyze and think about a problem allow you to think through the various scenarios, which makes your advice heartfelt and in most cases, accurate;

- You find you really like to create. You may not be crafty per se, but you like to apply your creativity to projects around the house. All of your alone time gives you all the time you need to really think about what you want, plus the time to make it happen;

- You are not big on social media. You don't like to advertise your personal life and prefer to be a silent observer. Some people may say you are extremely private or even a little mysterious. It is more that you prefer to keep to yourself and don't want or need strangers' opinions about your life choices;

- You have often been told you are too intense or you need to relax. This is a common introvert character trait. You are deemed intense because you are constantly evaluating a situation. You are not one to jump in with both feet until you have weighed all of the options;

- You like to observe and watch an activity before trying it yourself. This may also apply to work situations. You prefer to watch what others are doing before diving in. You are watching and learning from them so you are better prepared and have learned a lot from their mistakes;

- You prefer to invite a few people to your house for dinner or hanging out rather than going to their houses. This gives you the ability to control the situation more and you are more comfortable in your own surroundings;

- If you are at a loud party or an overly-stimulating situation, you tend to drift off. Your mind carries you to a place that is quiet. People will tell you that you have zoned out or ask you where you have gone. It is a self-protecting mechanism that you employ, often unknowingly to help you cope with too much going on around you.

If you can identify with more than 12 of these, you are an introvert. You are someone who is most comfortable at home, surrounded by your books and hobbies. Going out to a busy mall, wild parties or loud concerts is not your idea of a good time.

What isn't mentioned above is some of the perceived downsides to being an introvert. You may feel like you are always being passed over for promotions or your ideas are not taken seriously, even though you put a lot of time into researching and planning each one.

You may feel like, because you are not a social butterfly and chatting up the boss or your teacher, you are ignored.

You watch as your co-workers and others seem to jump over you and move past you, when you are the one with the good ideas. You have an excellent work ethic, but you just don't flaunt it like others. You don't have that smooth way of talking or the charisma that seems to come so naturally to others. This can lead you to feel left out, ignored and unappreciated.

You need to develop your charisma so your ideas are heard and you are taken more seriously.

You don't have to be the loudest person in the room or have the most friends to be successful. It is nothing more than a combination of your very strong, positive introvert character traits combined with a little charisma.

Chapter 2

Positive Mindset

Now that you know for sure you are an introvert or possess introvert qualities, you can start moving forward.

It is time to start building up your charisma so you can start feeling more accomplished. You will feel more fulfilled and you will love the way you are able to talk to others and share your ideas. We just established an introvert is full of creative ideas that will work. The problem is getting them out there and heard.

But, wait. What is charisma?

Charisma, by official definition means; compelling attractiveness or charm that can inspire devotion in others.

Doesn't that sound magical? Who wouldn't want to possess such a quality? It gives you visions of people hanging on your every word and willing to go to bat for you, no matter how ridiculous your idea sounds. This is the quality that some people seem to ooze. They walk into a room and everyone stops to hear what they have to say.

You may admire this quality in someone at work. Maybe it is your boss. Maybe it is your sibling who has always been able to attract oodles of friends without even trying.

The attractiveness isn't necessarily a physical trait or beauty by society's standards.

No, the attractiveness referenced in the definition is referring to the soul. A person's genuine nature or willingness to help others is an attractive quality that will draw people in.

Charisma is all about commanding the attention of others, without even trying. Someone who is charismatic doesn't need to convince another person to accept an idea. They have such a presence about them that it just happens, naturally.

Is charisma something you need?

Technically, probably not. Is it helpful and a desirable trait? Absolutely!

The thing is that charisma isn't necessarily something you are born with. For some, sure; it seems like they came out of the womb ready to charm everybody that passed by. That doesn't mean you can't develop your own brand of charisma that will help you get ahead in life.

Now, as an introvert you may be saying, "I'm okay with what I have. I don't need anything else."

You don't have to set a goal to be a millionaire or to own your own Fortune 500 company. That isn't what this is about. This is about you feeling like you are heard. Like you are being taken seriously. Feeling as if you can effect change for the better.

And guess what. As an introvert, you are quite capable of coming up with a life-changing product. It could even be world-changing. Your introvert tendencies give you a creative edge that may be lacking in extroverts.

They also make it possible for you to sit and daydream all alone and think of the various ways you could make things better. Take a moment to look around you. How many things are in your home right this very minute that make your life easier?

We are talking some of the most ridiculous things, like the little plastic tips on the end of your shoelaces to keep them from fraying.

Every day, we are blessed to reap the benefits of introverts that have put their ideas to work. Yes, they benefited and, yes, they probably got rich. It isn't so bad to be successful.

You may be thinking, "No, no, no, I don't want any recognition. I don't want people talking to me and what not." Look, you don't have to have your face splashed all over advertising and magazines. You can still be you, sitting at home (albeit a much nicer home) doing what you love most. In fact, you would have more freedom to hang out at home or in your hobby room because you allowed your charismatic self to get you ahead and earn you a nice income.

It isn't always going to be about money; I know. However, success is often linked to money. It doesn't mean it has to change you. It also doesn't guarantee you will actually get rich. Personal successes look different for each of us. Your idea of success may not be the same as your best friend's or even your closest sibling's.

A couple of psychologists have put some serious time and energy into studying charisma and how it helps or hurts people. They have determined charisma is a power. Not quite a super power, but something referred to as a referent power.

Referent power is described as; influence that you have because other people like and respect you.

Charisma is also useful in any social setting. You will feel more at ease talking with others. In fact, your words will be listened to and hung on. Introverts are such deep thinkers that they almost always have something of value to add to a conversation, but they are often ignored or not heard simply because they do tend to be quiet.

Charisma is the tool you need to really express your thoughts and opinions.

There are several very good, valid reasons you want and need charisma in your personal and professional life.

- You will appear confident, which will eventually lead to you feeling confident. Part of the reason introverts are not taken seriously is because they appear timid and shy when they are presenting an idea or solution. They don't seem to really believe in what they are saying. Charisma gives you that confidence that makes you sound authoritative;

- Charisma gives you the ability to engage others in your ideas and planning. You will have the confidence to bring people on board. People will appreciate you noticing them and, because of your charismatic presence, they are going to be happy to oblige;

- With newfound confidence comes newfound purpose. Charisma is a lot like an adrenaline rush. You will see clearer and be able to focus completely on your project or goal without necessarily blocking the rest of the world out. You have a goal and you are determined to reach it. You have been able to articulate the goal, which helps breathe life into it;

- Charisma gives you this magical ability to paint a clear picture for others to see. Your use of eloquent words that bring your ideas to life are going to have people flocking to you. They will want to be a part of your vision.

Because you are unique, charisma may look a little differently on you than it does on someone else.

We all have our strengths. You may be better at painting the picture of your vision while some other charismatic person may be better in the actual leadership area. **The key is to know your**

strengths and tap into them. You don't have to be great at everything, but you do need to have the confidence to maximize the things you are great at.

You may have an icky feeling about some charismatic people and that is normal. Some people ooze charisma and they use it to their sole advantage. A pushy salesperson who manages to talk you into buying something you didn't want or need may have charisma in spades, but they are using it for evil. Well, not evil, but they are using it to do bad, rather than good. They are using it to personally get ahead at the expense of someone else.

That is not the kind of charisma you want to develop or enhance.

Charisma can go either way. Let's assume you plan to develop your charisma to help others while helping yourself feel better and do better in the game of life. It is all about balance. Smooth talking a little old lady out of her retirement fund may be an excellent demonstration of charisma, but it is wrong. Charisma should be used to better the world—or at least your little corner of the world.

Now, you can certainly get ahead or be the leader of your group or the CEO without charisma, but it won't be easy. You won't have that knack for inspiring loyalty quite the same way and you will struggle a lot more. Charisma isn't just for others. It is for you. It will further inspire you and your introverted qualities to do more and to be better. It will give you a healthy dose of self-confidence that will help you break the barriers that either you have imposed on yourself or others have imposed on you because you have allowed them to.

It is important you fully understand charisma and then determine why you want it.

Be careful you don't emulate someone else or decide you want to develop your charisma so you can be more like Bob. Bob may not be as happy as he puts on or he may be using charisma is a way that isn't conducive to your own personal beliefs and core values.

Charisma is a tool that can backfire if you use it incorrectly. It is important to understand that the right way to use charisma is to benefit the people you are working with or hoping to influence. Charisma isn't all about you. Sorry. You can't make yourself the focus of the charisma.

Now, if you happen to be a rockstar at the charisma thing, it is easy to fall into the ego trap of being extremely charismatic. People will be falling at your feet and that can lead to you taking the praise and adoration and sidelining the real purpose for your newfound charismatic ways.

Chapter 3

Rules for Small Talk

Empathy

Empathy is one of your strongest tools in communicating and forming meaningful connections with others. It is easy to come off as thoughtless or insensitive if your ability to experience and express empathy isn't well developed. When you are talking to someone, try to understand how they are feeling from their point of view. Even if what they are experiencing and talking about isn't something that you have gone through personally, and even if it isn't something that you understand all that well, it is still important to find some common ground and then use that to help you to empathize with the other person.

For example, if you find that you don't respond much if another person is obviously feeling very happy or sad, or if you give harsh, tone deaf responses to a friend whose dog has died—because they should have "expected" it, since dogs don't live as long as humans, then you might need to work on developing your emotional empathy.

It is also important to develop cognitive empathy, which involves trying to understand how someone is feeling from a more logical perspective. For example, if you get annoyed at someone else who is not as educated as you, simply because they don't know something that you think should be "obvious", you need to work on improving your cognitive empathy, and understanding that not everyone has had the same opportunities as you to advance their studies.

If possible, let go of any preconceived notions that you have about a person. When you start out the conversation with an open mind, it is easier to have some empathy with the speaker and to respond appropriately. Reading widely and on a wide range of topics is another great way to expose yourself to many different viewpoints and life experiences. Not everyone has the same reaction to events as you do, and it's important to recognize this and to try and learn about someone else's viewpoint, which can help to develop your empathy.

Of course, there may be times when the other person is going to talk about a topic, or say something, that you don't really agree with. This doesn't give you the right to just barge in and start talking over them or putting them down for their perspective. Instead, if you do disagree with that person, you can wait and construct an argument later that will respectfully respond to what they said.

Even if you do decide to counter what the speaker has said because you don't agree with them, this doesn't mean that you should close your mind and ignore their feelings. When it comes to any kind of communication, whether it is in the form of small talk or not, it is so important to keep an open mind to the opinions, emotions and views of others. Even if you don't end up agreeing with them completely, you may be able to learn a few things along the way.

Don't interrupt with your own solutions

We are taught as children not to interrupt other people when they are talking. But much of what we see on television and in popular culture shows that it is just fine to interrupt someone and put in your own solutions.

Interrupting is one of the worst things that you can do when trying to have a conversation, whether you are talking to someone you just met, or someone you have known for a long time. When you interrupt, it is sending the message that:

1. This isn't a conversation. I see it as a contest, and I plan to win it.

2. I don't have time to wait around for your opinion.

3. I don't really care what you think, but I think that you should listen to me.

4. What I have to say is way more relevant, accurate, or interesting compared to what you have to say.

5. I'm more important than you.

Making an effort not to interrupt the other person helps to keep the conversation at an even pace and to ensure that you actually hear what the other person is saying, rather than talking over them.

Any time that you are listening to someone talk about one of their problems or another issue affecting them, you should work hard to not just suggest solutions. Most people aren't really looking for advice because they just want to be able to talk and let off some steam. If they do want some solutions, they are going to specifically ask for it.

You need to listen and help the other person find their own answers. Somewhere down the line, if you are absolutely bursting with a great solution, at least ask the other person whether they would like to hear the idea first.

Wait until the speaker pauses before asking for any clarifications

When you don't really understand what someone is saying, it is fine to ask them questions to make sure that you understand what is going on. It is much better to ask them to backtrack or to ask some questions to make sure you fully understand what is going on, rather than just continuing the conversation and being confused the whole time.

But make sure that you don't interrupt the other person when you ask for clarification. Wait until there is a natural pause from the speaker. Then, you can ask something like: "Back up a second. I didn't understand what you just said about…" This allows you a chance to get clarification, but it also shows the other person that you were listening to them and that you really want to hear what they have to say.

Ask questions but stick to the topic

During a conversation, there may be many points that come up that can lead to a conversational tangent that gets things off track. For example, at lunch, a colleague starts telling you about their recent trip overseas. In the course of this talk, they mention visiting a mutual friend. This can lead you to ask questions about that one mutual friend, and soon the topic has moved off from the original discussion about all of the amazing places that your colleague saw on holiday.

There is nothing wrong with asking questions to explore different elements of a topic—in fact, this can often help a conversation to evolve and flow well—but try to keep things relevant and on the same topic that the other person wants, at least to start with. If you notice that the question you have asked is leading the speaker astray, then you should take the responsibility to get it back on track. This can make the person you are talking to feel like they still have control over the conversation, and it helps you to practice going with the flow.

Pay attention to some of the nonverbal cues

There is a lot that the other person can say with their words, but there is even more that the other person can say that is nonverbal. It is possible to

52

glean a lot of information from another person without them even saying a word. This can even happen over the phone, with the help of listening to the inflections in their voice.

There are a lot of different nonverbal cues that you can pay attention to, when it comes to having a face to face conversation with another person. You can see whether the other person is irritated, bored, or enthusiastic just by observing their body language, the sound of their voice, and the expression on their face. These are all clues that you shouldn't ignore.

When you are listening to someone else and trying to glean everything that they want to tell you, you must be careful of what else is being said below the surface of their words. What the other person is saying out loud will only convey a fraction of the message. The nonverbal cues are just as important.

Show some regular feedback to the speaker

When trying to connect with another person during a conversation, it is important to give regular feedback. If you just stand there passively looking like a blank slate, not responding to them in any way, it will make the other person feel as if they aren't getting through to you and they will start withdrawing from you.

It can help to mirror their posture and body language, for example. You can also show the speaker that you understand where they are coming from by saying things like: "I can see that you are confused", "What a terrible ordeal for you", or: "You must be thrilled" in response to their story. If you are talking to that person and you find their thoughts and feelings unclear, then you can simply go through and paraphrase the message, as you understand it, on an occasional basis.

From there, you can just nod and show that you understand them with the help of appropriate facial expressions. The idea here is to give the speaker proof on some level that you are listening and that you are still following along with them on their train of thought.

You need to be an active listener when you are using small talk. Too many times we get involved in our own thought processes and expectations about how a conversation should unfold, instead of letting it flow and evolve naturally. If two people meet who are doing the same thing, then the conversation will come to an awkward halt.

But when you become an active listener, you will find that you can learn so much. You can easily catch on to the topics that the other person is bringing up, you can understand and respond to the cues that they send, and ask interesting questions to propel the conversation. You can feed off that and keep the conversation going for much longer, without feeling worn out, worried, or strained to find more topics to discuss.

Curios

Now that you're aware of some potential topics to talk about, it's time to know exactly how you can pull it off and initiate the conversation. Note that even if you're knowledgeable about possible topics for small talks, you will still have a hard time pulling it off if you don't know exactly how to deliver it.

Ask open-ended questions

A lot of people prefer to talk about themselves, so tapping into this is a great way to initiate small talks then keep the conversation going. Open questions require explanations, instead of just a yes or a no response. They often start with what, who, how, where, why and when. Closed questions, on the other hand, begin with are/am/is, have, and do. An example of open question are what type of music do you love the most and why? This often requires an explanation, so you can do away with a simple yes or no as an answer. Since there's an explanation, you can respond and lengthen the conversation.

Refer to previous discussions

If you will be talking with someone whom you've already talked to before, then it would be best to have a mental list of topics that you talked about before. You can then continue talking about one. Some examples would be a bad news he shared to you, a project he's working on, or a recent achievement of his child. Aside from giving you an idea about what to talk about, it can also make the other party feel better, since this shows that you are actually paying attention to what he's saying. It shows him how good of a listener you are and that you care about the experiences and problems he shared with you. This can further encourage him to build a connection.

Ask questions that he can easily answer

To successfully initiate small talks, and ensure that the conversation will keep going, you need to make sure that you ask questions that the other party will never have a hard time answering or responding to. Keep in mind that there are certain questions that are extremely difficult to answer. If you want to engage someone, raise easy and interesting questions that he will definitely love to answer. This can help ensure that the conversation will flow even better and more smoothly, making the two of you feel more comfortable.

Be sensitive

You can't just bombard someone with questions without considering about whether he's willing to talk about the topic/s you're interested in. If you're asking him a question, make sure it's non-invasive. It should not be related to topics they don't want to discuss. For instance, there are those who may feel irritated or distressed if you ask them about issues that affect them personally. These include weight, inadequate qualifications or skills, relationship issues, etc. Be sensitive and thoughtful. Avoid talking about issues that will invade their privacy or make them feel bad about themselves.

Say the name of the person you're talking to from time to time

Aside from helping you remember his name, it's also a good way to show your respect and to make him feel comfortable. Referring to him using his name can make the conversation even more personal, intimate and real. This will establish more connection, so don't be surprised if you notice that the small talk you initiated actually turned into a smarter, deeper and more meaningful one.

Stay engaged

Make sure that you don't make yourself look bored when talking to someone. Make him feel like you are really engaged in the talk you've initiated and that you're interested about what he's saying. Show him how willing you are to keep the discussion going. Focus on him, as well. Ensure that your curiosity remains piqued, instead of trying to withdraw back to yourself. This tip is crucial if you want to retain a more comfortable and light conversation and make sure that it continues.

The good thing about keeping yourself engaged during the entire duration of talking to someone is that it will give you ideas about the topics to talk about in your future small talks and conversations. This is especially true if you're going to talk to the same person again. This will instantly give you a hint about what you could possibly discuss about, such as asking for an update about a certain aspect in his life.

Be natural

When initiating small talks, you don't have to force yourself to act like someone you're not as this can only make you feel too uncomfortable. Be natural. Respond to situations based on how you normally do. Laugh and smile naturally each time someone makes a joke or funny remark. Avoid forcing laughter, though, as this may alarm him. Smile and nod naturally. Be yourself and you will most likely bring out these reactions naturally, instead of making them look forced and awkward.

Don't worry too much about pauses

There's nothing to worry in case there are some pauses after you've talked about a certain topic. The good thing about pauses is that you can actually use them to change topics. These also serve as a way to take a short break or breather and re-energize the small talk. There's nothing to worry about unless the pause and silence is already too long. Avoid stressing yourself because as long as you excuse yourself for a while, or move naturally into the next subject, then you're all good.

Don't be afraid to get a little more personal

This is a useful tip, provided you determine first if the other party is willing to talk about something personal. One advantage of getting more personal, with the consent of the other person, is that you get the chance to get closer to him more quickly. You can easily become more familiar about him, making it easier to build a connection. Some safe topics, despite being a bit personal, that you can talk to him about could be his favorite book, his favorite sports team, his passion and hobbies, and his favorite holiday.

Ask follow-up questions

Once you've initiated a small talk, be sure to pay attention to his responses. This is a huge help in weaving good follow-up questions. Your follow-up questions will also keep the conversation going. Just make sure that you don't probe too much to avoid annoying him. Your questions should still be answerable by something, which he finds comfortable in.

Avoid making your small talk partner uncomfortable, as well. Be sensitive on his responses – be it verbal or non-verbal. It's also advisable to be more respectful in your response to someone who stays uncomfortable or awkward with you around. If the person you're talking to seems uninterested to share details or info or seems withdrawn, then avoid persisting too much.

While asking follow-up questions is essential in keeping the talk going, learn when to stop. Avoid asking too many questions if he starts to become unresponsive.

Listen

Small talk can be a lot of work for many people who don't like trying to think about inconsequential topics to keep the conversation going. They may be uncomfortable with getting the other person to start talking, and they want to make sure that they don't say anything that is going to offend the other person or to cause a big lull in the conversation.

One of the keys that you can work on to make sure that you can get small talk to work well, is to listen. The more that you can listen and gather from the other person, the easier it is to keep the conversation flowing.

Here are some of the key skills that you need to use in order to practice active listening, so that small talk will be more effective for you:

Don't do all the talking

It is common to get nervous when talking to others. To avoid any silence when the conversation comes to a stop, we may overcompensate and start to talk aimlessly, barely letting the other person talk at all.

If you don't pause to allow a natural back-and-forth, then you risk turning the conversation into a monologue. The good news about active listening is that you don't have to talk too much, as you encourage the other person to do most of the talking.

This doesn't mean that you should just stand there and say nothing the whole time. But if you use active listening to bring up the right questions, you may be able to keep the conversation going for quite some time, without really having to do much talking at all.

For example, you can ask more questions about the topic at hand; you can ask for clarification; and then you can ask a few more questions to bring the conversation back up again when needed. Talking is important but try to get the other person to do a lot of talking, while you listen, as much as possible.

Try to put the speaker at ease

When you start small talk with a new person, whether you have met them before or it is the first time that you have ever spoken to them, try to put them at ease as quickly as possible. It is natural for both you and for them to be a bit nervous by the situation, but if you are able to put the other person at ease, then you are going to feel more at ease as well.

Your job here is to try to help the other person feel like they are open and free to speak about anything that they want. Remember their concerns and needs, and listen to what they have to say. Make sure that you use nods or other gestures and words to encourage the other person to continue with what they are saying, and to show that you are truly interested.

Eye contact can be so important here. Do not look at the floor, look at your hands, or look at other things that are going on around you. This is going to send out the wrong message, and makes the other person feel like you are bored with them, or that there are more important things for you to focus your attention on.

Strong eye contact, without staring and seeming aggressive, is so important. You need to look the other person in the eyes, while smiling and appearing attentive, to show that what they have to say is important and you are listening, understanding, and appreciating the conversation.

Find ways to remove distractions

There are always going to be a lot of distractions that show up in the world around you. Whether it is from your phone beeping, from others walking around, and even from your email. But if you let yourself get distracted by all these things, then your attention is taken away from the conversation at hand. How are you supposed to be effective at engaging in small talk, or any kind of communication, if you are so distracted that you can't even hear what the other person is saying?

When you are working on your listening skills, make sure that all the distractions are put away. Turn off the computer, the phone, and the television, to make sure that there is no chance that they will get in the middle of the conversation.

Don't look out the window, pick at your fingers, shuffle papers, or doodle. This kind of distracted behavior sends a message to the other person that you are bored or disinterested in them and what they have to say. If your roles were reversed, how would that make you feel?

If you can, it is also important to avoid any interruptions. While you may not be able to avoid these all the time—for example, if you are at a party and someone walks over and interrupts, there isn't much you can do—you can try to avoid them as much as possible.

You want to make sure that you can put your full attention on the speaker, and that you make them feel at ease and like the most important person around. You can't do that if you are constantly checking your email on your phone, looking out the window, or looking around the room.

Chapter 4

How to Start a Conversation With

People dislike being lonely, and if they sense that they can feel less alone by engaging another person in a simple conversation, then they will. A lot of shy people tend to feel alone because they cannot find the courage to talk to another person, even if they are sharing the same space. However, there are certain social conventions that might be the cause of anxiety, conventions that prompt one to think that it is difficult to deal with other people and that one is much safer without inviting a new person into one's life. After all, most shy people have been let down by others at some point, and it is an act of self-preservation to be anxious around strangers.

Strangers

Solitude can be unhealthy for some, and it can even make one feel that he or she is unprepared for "battle." When shy kids enter school, for example, they are forced into social interaction at a level that is unprecedented for most children at that age, making them engage in a battle armed with a gun, but no bullets. Some children can become cynically shy. In other words, they may feel so disconnected from the rest of the world that they become hostile towards others. In a world where everybody seems to want to make connections, being left out can be utterly frustrating. A lot of shy people do try to connect with those around them, contrary to the belief that shyness is equivalent to passiveness. Those who are shy are excited to be invited to events, but they often feel depressed due to their perception that their preparation is incomplete, since after all, they cannot muster the courage to start a conversation. Some seek the courage to connect through lowering their inhibitions with alcohol and drugs, a solution that is temporary at best, not to mention potentially fatal.

People are encouraged to talk to others in order to prevent feelings of hate and animosity towards others who belong in social groups. At the end of the day, everyone wants to feel belongingness and acceptance, as well as to feel that the world is a safe place.

friends

Once you make it past the introductions and the first few generic conversational lines, you must find a way to distinguish yourself from others who might, at first glance, seem rather similar.

If your newfound potential friends never learn anything distinctive about you, due either to your own shyness or to conversations simply never getting passed the most mundane of topics, it is unlikely that you will ever develop a deeper connection with them. There would simply be no way for them to know if the two of you have anything in common worth pursuing, any shared interests that you may want to delve into a deeper conversation about one day. They will be unaware of your strengths, your weaknesses, your quirks and your charms. Of course, this is hardly information you need to display openly to anyone and some traits might very well be best kept firmly under wraps until true intimacy is established but revealing select tidbits that might prove interesting can allow you to build and enhance new friendships by opening up about yourself. In turn, your new companions will be more inclined to do the same, possibly revealing shared eccentricities, interests or lifestyle choices that you can enjoy and/or discuss together in more detail.

Often, the biggest detriment to letting others see glimpses of our personality and interests is due to shame. What if they dislike those features or interests, and we simply embarrass ourselves? What if they consider the information we share out of place or too forward and everything is awkward between them and us forever? All too often we convince ourselves that the things we like and our own personalities will not be liked by others, but the only way to know is to let prospective friends know about these things. If you hide them, you will be rather bland since none of your best personality features or fun interests will be shown at all. You will also eliminate the chance of learning if they might enjoy similar pastimes or share your quirks and that would be a shame because shared interests and features are a surefire way to trigger bonding and a memorable impression.

As for technique on how to accomplish this, it is actually fairly straightforward. If something comes up that interests or excites you, simply mention it. Ask your acquaintance their thoughts on it and share yours. In this way, you can discuss skills, hobbies, even qualities you possess or value in others in a relatively organic way. Be careful not to force your viewpoints upon your chat companion. Express yourself in an enthusiastic but non-judgmental manner. You might discover that you have a lot in common, but the reverse could also happen. Even if you discover that you have little in common with the person who was so recently a stranger, it will do you little good to burn bridges or create an enemy. If you discover that your opinions diverge in a manner too significant to move past pleasantly, change the topic or if you must, politely end the conversation. If on occasion someone does hold different values or simply does not seem to share any of your interests, do not take it personally. In many cases, if you approach such people with flexibility and genuine interest, you might find that you have more in common than you thought or at the very least you will gain an interesting new perspective. Ultimately, no harm is likely to befall you from making your own interests and personality traits apparent, the worst case scenario, you simply both move on, leaving your own mentalities firmly intact. In other scenarios, you may be able to enjoy conversing with even someone with very different viewpoints from your own once you understand the reasoning behind them. Do not let fears of shame, judgment or rejection keep you from letting others see who you really are. It is the only way you can have valid and legitimate conversations with others, and that is worth the relatively minor risk incurred.

Colleagues

When running into a long-lost friend, colleague, or acquaintance, you can be more informal. Even a simple, "Hello! How are you? It's been a long time" will start the conversation, perhaps even lead to a longer conversation or a future hookup. Still, it doesn't hurt to know these tips to ensure that an accidental meeting can become productive and pleasant.

☐ Show your enthusiasm for the meeting. You can say, "It's been forever! How are you?" or "I haven't seen you for so long! What's up?"

☐ Smile and make eye contact, too. You may either shake hands or hug each other depending on your past relationship, although a physical touch isn't mandatory in all cases.

☐ Listen to the information shared by your friend and offer your own personal information, too. But keep it brief since there's little need to go into the gory details of your life. Ask about other members of the family, if you're familiar with them, too, since it shows your concern and extends the conversation.

You don't have to share details if you aren't comfortable with it. Just say, "Oh, nothing special, just the usual work-study-home routine" or "Same old, same old." You may, nonetheless, have to offer just a little bit more if the other person

72

graciously offered a tidbit of information about what's up with his/her life.

End the small talk with an invitation to spend time in the future, which may or may not be definite. You can say, "Let's get together for coffee sometime," but you don't necessarily have to ask for the other person's contact details or give yours unless you're being asked for it. You can give your social media account, or your cellphone number, or your email address, whichever suits your mood at the moment.

Chapter 5

Example of Small Talk

Small talk isn't small, no matter what one might think. You may think that talking about the weather is clichéd, but many a great relationship or friendship has started over shared frustrations about this innocuous subject. Small talk isn't just a means of filling in uncomfortable silences. It is a way to build bonds with people and a skill that can be absolutely vital in the professional arena. If you want to become an expert at small talk, here are some steps you need to keep in mind.

Make Your Body Language Approachable

If you want someone to feel comfortable around you, pay attention to your stance. Don't come on too strong, but do move your body towards the person. Make eye contact, turn your torso towards them but don't cross your arms over your chest. Don't stand too close or too far. Doing all this will make the person feel as though you're interested in what they have to say and aren't just tolerating them.

Another non-verbal cue that makes people feel you're not paying attention is constantly looking at your phone. It gives the impression that what you're looking at there is more interesting than what they have to say.

At the same time, give the other person their space. As I said earlier, don't stand too close. Look eager to listen to what they have to say, but not so eager that it borders on manic. You don't want to scare the person away.

Have a Friendly Greeting Ready

Your greeting depends, of course, on whether you know the person or not. If it is someone you're already acquainted with a simple hello followed by his or her name will do. For example, "Hey John, how are you?" It's direct and simple and let's them know that you're interested in talking to them. If it's someone you're meeting for the first time, start by introducing yourself. It'll help you feel confident. You can say something like, "Hi, I'm John. May I know your name?" Once the introduction is complete, repeat the other person's name; it's a great way to remember names and it makes them feel special.

Smile when the two of you are talking and ensure that you pay attention to them when you greet them. Do not look bored or perform perfunctory introductions as though you were just waiting for someone more interesting to show up.

Talk Lightly and Positively

You exchange energy in a conversation just as much as you do information. To ensure that you have great small talk that can lead to a great conversation, keep things fun, positive and light. A positive and upbeat attitude and a willingness to laugh at funny parts of the conversation, especially when they're about you, makes another person want to keep talking to you even when you're discussing something as mundane as the weather.

Of course, fun and light is difficult after a bad day at work or at home. However, if you're engaging in small talk with someone, chances are they aren't a close friend. Letting go and complaining about how bad your day, week, month or year has been will only succeed in turning them off.

Begin with a Compliment

Start with a basic compliment such as, "I really like your skirt – where did you get it?" Before you know it, you may be involved in a fun conversation about retail therapy. Don't be disheartened if the conversation doesn't immediately take off, though. You've still appreciated something about that person, which will make them feel good about themselves and therefore, about you. They will be more receptive to other subjects that you talk about. If you're feeling a bit leery about leading straight in with an introduction, you can use this as a way to introduce yourself.

Figure Out What You Have in Common

Establishing common ground doesn't just mean that both of you are fans of the same sports team. Something as commonplace as having the same bad experiences with traffic that day can be used to discover common ground. Common ground is simply a way to establish what both of you can relate to, so that a connection can be formed. You may find the weather too innocuous or cliché to talk about, but remember that you can build up to the stuff that matters once you have established common ground. Here are some ways to do this:

"Isn't Professor Duncan funny?"

"Don't you just love the parties that Justin throws?"

"Did you also get stuck in the rain today?"

"Glen's Kitchen is one of my favorite places to hang out."

Open Up a Bit about Yourself

Now that common ground has been established, you can use it as a basis to open up a bit about yourself. This doesn't mean that you tell them something intensely personal that will probably scare them off such as, "I'm so obsessed with Professor Duncan." However, you can use this opportunity to talk about yourself a little bit more. Here are some ways to follow up on the statements in the previous point:

"I enjoy his classes immensely. He makes archaeology sound like fun."

"I met Justin last week when I was doing an interview with one of the other players."

"I tried to set out early to beat the weather, so I could get to the gym but I was too late. I had to spend the next one hour in traffic."

"I find that it's the best place to hangout with my friends. The music isn't too loud so you can hear yourself talk and they do a mean pizza with barbecue sauce."

Engage the Other Person

Establishing common ground and opening up about yourself is just one step. Now you need to bring the other person into the conversation. You can do this by asking them to yield some information about themselves. Don't ask intensely personal questions such as their viewpoint on religion or politics. Keep it simple and fun. Ask questions about their job, interests or even surroundings. Here are a few ways to engage another person:

"What about you? Are you interested in archaeology too, or do you enjoy his jokes?"

"Have you been to any of Justin's parties before or are you attending one for the first time?"

"Did the rain keep you from something fun today?"

"Do you come here to hang out or for the food?"

Ask a Question or Make a Statement

Your next step will depend upon how the person responds. Below are a few ways to keep a conversation going:

Other person: "Oh, I'm an archaeology student too. Duncan's a bonus, but I've always wanted to be an archaeologist."

You: "Really? What drew you to archaeology? It's great to meet someone who is as interested as I am in this field."

Other person: "It's my first time attending one of Justin's parties but I've heard of them. I heard the Halloween party was a blast."

You: "Oh it was! So how do you know Justin?"

Other person: "I like the rain but not when I'm planning to head out for a movie. Missing that movie was a real letdown."

You: "What movie were you going for?"

Other person: "I love the food here. While I enjoy the pizza, I especially love their mushroom pot pie."

You: "Oh yes! The mushroom pot pie is delicious. Have you tried out any other dishes they make?"

Use Your Surroundings

Once the conversation really gets going, you can look for cues around you if you're stuck about what to say next. Use anything that you see – from what they might be wearing to posters on the wall. Here are some examples:

"This Coldplay t-shirt is so cool. Did you enjoy the concert?"

"Hey, you participated in the Ironman too? When? How was that experience?"

"Do you think this rendition of Macbeth will be good? I've been wanting to see the play for some time."

"Oh wow! You're reading 'The Picture of Dorian Grey'? Doesn't that book have interesting things to say about man's true nature?"

Listen Carefully to Them

Paying close attention or 'listening actively' to what the other person is saying can give you more cues about how to make the conversation lively and productive. If you hear a small comment that has the potential to take the conversation in a new direction, use it. Here are a few examples of how to use tangential cues in a conversation:

You: "I met Justin while holidaying with some common friends in France."

Other person: "Justin told me about that trip. He actually wanted a few lessons in French before setting out on it, although I don't know how much French he actually ended up using."

You: "Do you speak French? That is so cool. Where did you learn it?"

Other person: "My mother is from Quebec actually, so her first language is French. I learnt it at her knee. It's very different from the French spoken in New Orleans though, isn't it?"

You: "So I've heard. I believe that some expressions that are completely harmless in Parisian French can be considered quite offensive there. But I love the Fat Tuesday the best! New Orleans can be so much fun right?"

Other person: "Oh yes! It truly believes in letting the good times roll."

You: "Have you ever been there? How was it?"

Reveal Something of Yourself, Not Everything

By the time the conversation ends, you could have told the other person a bit more about yourself such as your volunteer work at animal shelters, how much you like videos of Gatsby the dog, or even how you feel about the latest Oscar winning movies. The person leaves having gained an insight into you that can forge a deeper connection and doesn't make them believe that the conversation wasn't important to you.

At the same time, though, be careful about how much you say. This isn't the time to talk about your political or religious views, your love life or your latest existential crisis.

If the Conversation Goes Well, Suggest Meeting Again

If the conversation has gone well so far, you will probably want to follow up with this person. This is when you can ask for their number or whether they want to hang out again.

"I would love to go see that play with you. Could I have your number so we plan it out?"

"I've never met someone who has enjoyed Fat Tuesday as much as I have. Do you want to hang out again so we can talk?"

"Will I see you at Justin's next party? I hear the theme is New Orleans so it should be quite a blast."

Farewell Pleasantly

After the small talk is over and you have to go, ensure that you leave the person feeling important and not as though you were just passing the time with them. Here are some ways to say goodbye politely and nicely.

"I had a lot of fun talking to you. I'll let you know how my next trip to NOLA goes."

"I'd love to discuss the book further but I see a friend who's about to leave."

"There's a classmate, Julian. Do you know him? Come with me and I'll introduce the two of you."

Ending A Conversation Positively

No matter how swimmingly your conversation is going, all good things must come to an end and eventually that will include your discussions. Sometimes, this can feel awkward, with both members of the conversation needing or wanting to tend to someone else but each of us feeling pressured by social norms to avoid being rude and cutting someone off. started, and we will delve into those strategies in this chapter.

If you feel it is time to end a conversation, do so politely but firmly. In many cases a not entirely subtle sign that you need to start doing other tasks will work but if you have a particularly chatty companion mere hints might not work. You can certainly start with a nice and simple "While I would love to chat more, I really have to get going." You can be more specific here if possible such as tell them you have to go to work, an appointment or any other obligation that you were going to tend to before the conversation. Do not make excuses just to end a discussion so honestly divulge the reason behind the departure in an upbeat and friendly manner. If your chatting mate does not seem to grasp that by mentioning your need to go accomplish other tasks, you are trying to let them know that it is time to say your farewells, you will have to be a bit more direct. Remain cordial and do not grow terse with them but be firm if they continue talking. "I hope we can continue this conversation soon, but I truly must get some work done. I will talk to you again later." In many cases, you can then simply wave and head off in whatever direction you need to go. You want to ensure that they do not have a good opportunity to interject and keep you from ending the chat.

The methods discussed in the previous paragraph also can work wonders when both parties are aware that the conversation is at an end, but both feel too shy to properly end it. If you find yourself in a scenario where both members are dropping hints about all of the things that they still need to attend to that day and neither is simply saying goodbye, be the one to take that step. As before, be friendly but firm. Assure your new acquaintance that you would be delighted to continue your chat at another time but you both have things to do for the rest of the day, and you will, unfortunately, have to postpone such pleasantries for an alternate date or time.

If you are ever in an event where your conversation partner needs to go and excuses themselves, try to pick up on their own hints and conclude your conversation. Otherwise, things can sometimes grow terse, and there is a risk that you will be cut off rather bluntly while they return to their own affairs. Additionally, prolonging goodbyes and making someone feel pressured into continuing to talk to you is unlikely to leave them with a positive impression overall. They will feel annoyed and might also second guess themselves if they feel that they were rude by ending a conversation you were not yet ready to finish. When attempting to make friends and master small talk, it is preferable to avoid putting anyone in such a situation. If they seem like they would like to end the conversation, offer to talk again later, wish them well and go about your business. They are sure to appreciate it and think well of you going forward.

Finally, it is prudent to end a conversation before it becomes stale. If you are starting to run out of topic ideas and foresee awkward silences incoming, conclude the conversation while you are ahead. Even if you might like to communicate more, if you are out of content that naturally fits into your conversation and relationship level, it is better to end the conversation and talk again in the future. Your topic choices will expand as you get to know each other more, and even some rehashing will likely be comfortable for everyone and not overly stale. Additionally, if you sense a vastly different opinion in the conversation that could become potentially confrontational, or you inadvertently unearth an uncomfortable or overly controversial topic choice, you might be wise to conclude your chat before it becomes a debate. When you are communicating with someone you do not know too well, some cans of worms are not worth opening right away, lest you jeopardize a potential friendship or connection. If you are able to ensure that you finish your discussions before things get tense, boring or awkward, you are sure to have pleasantly concluded conversations for years to come, and that will be the ending impression of you that people carry with them, making them desire to speak with you again in the future.

Chapter 6

How to Build a Relationship as an Introvert

As an introvert, you may find that making new friends is not always as easy as it can be for others. Introverts like to go more for quality when picking out their friends, rather than quantity. So, while some people are interested in going all out and having as many friends as possible, introverts tend to be more selective and picky, and will only choose friends that really understand them, who share the same interests, and who are willing to accept them as they are.

If an introvert is not able to share their innermost thoughts, secrets, and dreams with another person, then they are never really going to consider that other person their friend. They may see this person as a nice acquaintance, or someone they like a lot, but not really a true friend. Because of this desire for more depth and quality in their friendships, the introvert is perfectly fine having just one or two friends.

Of course, this doesn't mean that introverts aren't allowed to have a large number of friends if they want. Some introverts are more sociable and thrive with a larger number of friends. But this doesn't mean that they are going to run out and get more friends just to say that they have them.

However, introverts will often find that it is harder for them to develop the high-quality friendships that they are looking for. They have trouble when it comes to reaching out to new people, and even when they do, it is hard for them to find someone they "click" with.

The issue here is that all humans, whether they are introverts or extroverts, are made to be in society and to seek out relationships. In fact, there are many studies out there that show that being social and having close relationships with others increases the mental and physical health of the individual, along with their overall happiness. But a lack of close friendships, and some of the isolation that comes with this, can have the exact opposite effect.

Despite the belief that most introverts don't even like other people, these individuals need human connection, just like everyone else does. But they are going to have some different needs when it comes to their relationships.

A good way to think about the emotional needs of an introvert, compared to an extrovert, is that they are fine having other people around and in the same house, but they don't want a lot of people in the same room as them all the time. They are fine with people, but they get energy from spending time on their own, without other people being on top of them.

However, the world around them is not always going to be the most conducive to this ideal. The world is often going to be loud and in-their-face—and sitting next to someone in silence isn't really going to create much of a lasting friendship. It is important to remember that introverts are just as able to create some of the human connections that they need, but sometimes they need to step away from their own comfort zones in order to make this happen.

There are some things that you can do in order to make it easier to find friends, even when you are an introvert. It actually isn't as hard as you may think.

If you don't have the energy to reach out to others, find ways to draw them to you

As an introvert, there are going to be times when you are too worn out, or too uncomfortable, to go around and try to make small talk to find new friends. You may get into a room full of people, and just want to scurry the other way. This is fine. It is okay to not always have the energy that is needed to be overly social and to be out there chasing down others and trying to do all the work to form the connections you need.

This doesn't mean that you should give up. It just means that you should find other ways to get this done. One method that can be just as effective, if not better, is to find a way to draw others to come to you, rather than you going to them. The idea of a smile can go a long way here too.

No matter what mood you are in, no matter how tired you are, and no matter what circumstances are going on around you ahead of time, make sure that your ultimate goal is to smile as much as possible.

Let's say that you are at a party and you see someone else walk into the room. If you make eye contact with them and smile at them, they are going to notice you, and maybe even come over to talk. That is, if they are interested in making a connection themselves. If they don't come over, then you can just keep going with the things you were doing before. If they do come over, you have created a friendly start to meeting someone new, and all you had to do was smile. You can greet them warmly and they will most likely start a conversation and try to keep it going, and you can just go along for the ride.

It isn't always your job to charm others

Shy introverts can feel a lot of pressure in social settings to be outgoing, vivacious, and charming, fearing that there is no way that another person will ever like them or become their friend. When they try to be charming or outgoing, it usually doesn't go all that well. Often, they will struggle and get their words jumbled, or get lots of nervous laughter, and the situation just gets more uncomfortable for them as it goes on.

The thing to remember here is that there isn't really a rule in place that says you absolutely need to be a charmer to have any hope of making connections. Instead of working so much on charming others, or trying to behave the way that an extrovert would, work on being confident in yourself. Learn how to be self-assured in the things that you appreciate and stand for; for the interests and values that you have; and in who you are.

There is nothing wrong with being "the quiet one" when out in a social setting. Sure, there is a lot of push back in our world against this, where people think that you need to be outgoing and act a certain way, but this just isn't the way that most introverts work.

When you are ready to reach out to another person, then go ahead and do it. If you don't, then don't pressure yourself. If someone does start to approach you, don't feel nervous. If you feel confidence in who you are as a person, and your innate likeability, then it doesn't matter what the other person thinks of you, or if there are awkward moments in your conversation. The more comfortable you are with not being the life of the party, and the less you try to change your personality, the more likely it is that you can actually start to enjoy yourself and attract the kind of people and friendships that will be best for you.

It is fine to be vulnerable on occasion

For many introverts, it is sometimes hard to be vulnerable. Many of these individuals like to keep to themselves, and they strive to showcase a perfect persona to everyone they come across. But when building friendships, think of these words from C.S. Lewis: "Friendship is born at the moment when one person says to another: 'What! You too? I thought I was the only one...'" This moment is not going to happen between you and another person unless you can be courageous enough to open yourself up.

The deeper that you are willing and able to go into these new friendships, the more meaning there is going to be behind them. Building up to revealing a healthy amount of vulnerability is going to need to start somewhere. Why can't it start with you? Showing someone else that you are willing to be honest and open gives them permission to be honest and open as well. You can both feed off each other in this way, in a cycle that will create a deeper bond than before.

There are a lot of ways that you can show some vulnerability to another person. When you are meeting someone new, you can keep it simple. You don't have to introduce yourself and then start talking about all your biggest fears in the first five minutes.

Some examples of how to initially show some vulnerability could include the following admissions:

1. "I really wish that there were some people I knew at this gathering."
2. "Do you know any good ice breakers? I've never been really good at them."
3. "I don't know about you, but I really am not a fan of these kinds of big parties."

After you have had a chance to talk with someone for a while, or maybe met up with them more than once, it is time to build up the relationship some more. The way that you show more vulnerability will change as the relationship develops. Some examples of things that you can say to show your vulnerability as you are starting to build up these new relationships, include:

1. "I start to feel pretty anxious when I get to a new class."
2. "I like hanging out with you."
3. "I'm having some trouble with [fill in the problem here]. Can I have a few minutes to vent to you?"
4. "I really appreciate the way that you have been supporting me."

It is so important to be vulnerable with another person if you are going to be friends. Friends should be those people who you feel comfortable to share personal life with. If you just want to work on outward appearances forever and never really dig into any of the things that matter to you, then you are just acquaintances. But when you open up and allow yourself to be vulnerable a little bit, then you are going to find that deeper bonds can begin to form.

Seek out other introverts like yourself

There is nothing wrong with picking out an extrovert to be your friend. They may help to get you out more socially and to experience different things in life, and they can be a lot of fun. This piece of advice isn't telling you to completely avoid making friends with extroverts. If you feel a connection with them, go for it.

But if all of your friends are extroverts, then it can sometimes be emotionally draining, since they will want to go out and be social all the time, while you crave some peace and quiet in your own home.

As an introvert, it is sometimes better for most of your friends to be introverts, and for you to look out for other introverts to spend time with. Any time that you do go out in a social setting, whether it is to a party, to a camp, or to school, etc. your goal should be to search out other introverts like yourself, who will likely understand you better and give you the space that you need.

There are a lot of benefits to picking out introverts as your friends. They aren't going to pressure you to change the way that you think or your personality. They won't try to turn you into a vivacious human when you aren't. So, how do you find these people? Look around the room and see if there is anyone who is quietly hanging out along the edges. Then you can make the first move and go and talk to them. It could be the start of a great new friendship.

Figure out the love language of the other person, and then share what yours is

Although the Five Love Languages are often geared towards relationships that are more romantic, they can be used in many other situations as well. Partners have used them to help understand each other better. Parents have used them to help understand their children and how to better raise them. And you can even use these love languages to deepen the friendships that you have.

There are some simple tests that you can take to figure out what your love language is, and then you can learn a bit more about the others as well. Not everyone is going to have the same love language as you. By assuming that everyone sees things the way that you do, you miss out on appreciating how unique each individual is, which can lead to disagreements and make it harder to form the deep connections that are needed.

There are five of these love languages to watch out for, and they include: physical touch; acts of service; words of affirmation; gifts; and quality time. We often find that we will give out love the same way that we want to receive it. But if the other person we are trying to connect with has a different love language, the desired effect is not going to be received.

For example, if "acts of service" is your love language, you may be more likely to run errands for the other person, help them clean up, or make them dinner. But if their love language is "physical touch", then there can be a disconnect. This doesn't mean that they won't appreciate the things that you do, it just won't lead to a deep connection. You need to meet them where their love language is, and they have to meet you where your love language is, in order to form those great connections.

The first step is to know your love language. Take a look at the five options listed above and see if any of them sticks out for you when it comes to how you react to other people and what behavior you appreciate the most from others. If you are uncertain, you can consider working with an online test to help you out. Once you know what your own love language is, you can then focus on the love language of those around you, making it easier for you to connect in a better and more effective, manner.

Hold out for the true connections, and don't try to settle

This is something that is going to come naturally for a lot of introverts, but it is never something that hurts to be reminded about. There is nothing quite like the moment of two souls meeting. You shouldn't just rush out and make friends with the first person you run across, unless you and that person are really able to click, and you feel a deeper connection with them. Hold out for a bit and see if you can find someone who really completes you, who really "gets" you, rather than just jumping on the first friendship opportunity that you find.

As an introvert, it is a good idea to hold out for a good friend. Hold out for someone who is going to make you feel safe and comfortable right away. Hold out for someone you feel that you can talk to about anything, without having to worry about them judging you. Hold out for someone who is able to make you happy.

It can take many introverts some time to open themselves up to others, because they are already so aware of their own internal lives. The good thing about this is that many times, they are able to get a quick sense about whether they connect with someone or not.

Introverts can get impatient when they aren't able to make those deep connections quickly. But remember that it is always worth it to hold out for that one in a million friend.

Be intentional

As an introvert, you are going to need to take some extra steps and precautions to ensure that you can reach out to other people. Many introverts may find that it is easy to get caught up in their own world, and then not talk to others for a long period of time. It may feel like they are ignoring other people, or that they don't really care, but in reality, they may lose sight of things or not even think about it.

It is important that you don't fall into this trap. You have to check in with your friends often, and this is going to get even more important the older that you get. Of course, it is also something that is going to get quite a bit harder—especially if you keep saying, "We should get together..." but then don't make it a priority as time goes by. Unfortunately, for many friendships, especially when they involve introverts, this can easily happen.

However, you will find that a little effort is going to go a long way. You don't have to make it something big or do a grand gesture each time you catch up. A simple text message to check in with the other person, a Skype or phone call, or a meetup or event planned in advance can all help you to maintain your friendships better, even when you are dealing with being separated by time or space.

It is going to take some work to make your friendships last. You need to make sure that you are intentional in setting up time to prioritize other people, even when it feels impossible or exhausting. When you are able to do this, you will find that it leads to relationships that are deeper and more meaningful, and this can do so much good for your mental, emotional, and physical wellbeing.

Chapter 7

From Basic Talk to Intimacy

Okay, so at this point you are probably aware of steps you can take to overcome your fear, take that first step and talk to someone. You should also now be knowledgeable of some of the strategies you can employ to make a memorable first impression showing off a taste of your interests and personality. But how do you communicate with someone past the first few interest getting lines and basic introductions? What enables people to move into more personal conversations and learn more about one another?

We will tackle the issue of how to take the next step past simple introductions with your new acquaintances in this chapter. If you have been following previous lessons, you will find that it is simpler than you might originally have expected. At this point in your conversation, you will have finished introducing yourself, perhaps pointed out something you found interesting about your new acquaintance and engaged in no more than a few sentences about relatively mundane things. From here, try to find a way to naturally spurn the conversation forward. If there is something pleasantly distinctive about your potential friend, ask about it. Compliments work well here but are too closed to ensure a good conversation. Do not just tell them you like their outfit but ask where they got it and if they regularly enjoy fashion. If something about their appearance or accessories suggests a shared interest, ask about it in a curious and enthusiastic manner now.

Moving to a more intimate stage is even easier when you are speaking to a coworker, classmate or anyone you met in a shared social event. You clearly have something in common binding you together. Ask your new colleague how they are enjoying the job so far and what they did before coming here. Asking classmates what they are studying is a common equivalent and for both groups of people you can ask them what they like (and even what they dislike) about their current or future line of work. Share your own feelings on the matter as well when it is your turn to speak. If you are at a recreational or leisure class or event, ask them how much experience they have with what you are doing and how they got into it in the first place.

If you are attempting to communicate fully with a stranger with whom you have no known like interests or tasks, it will take longer to build a connection. Ask simple and inoffensive things that can help you find shared things and show an interest. Are they from the town you are in and if not, where did they come from? In either case, do they like it here? Depending on the flow of the conversation, it might be natural to ask them briefly about their family or what they recommend doing for fun around the area. Step lightly when asking more personal questions, though, especially of someone who is more or less still a stranger to you. Read their body language and alter your questions if they appear uncomfortable. Do not be afraid to apologize if you feel you may have overstepped at some point. In doing so, you will show that you are paying attention to and listening to them and that you care about their comfort and happiness.

No matter how you meet someone, you can rest assured that the majority of people enjoy talking about themselves. Even if your initial conversational points are quite mundane, gently prodding for more information using thoughtful follow-up questions will usually enable you to get a conversation flowing and when that occurs you are likely to encounter a shared interest or trait. When you find one, mention it and ask for further information on their perspective on it. Very soon the conversation will flow naturally as two or more compatible people discuss a shared passion, and you will rapidly find yourself moving past mere introductions as you speak as friends do.

You get only one chance to make a first impression. Nowhere is this adage truer than it is on a first date. Naturally, you'll want to present yourself in the best possible light to ensure that things go favorably. It's not that difficult to do this and get a second date. Be considerate and polite to your date, display an interest in them and ensure that they enjoy their time with you. Honestly, that's all it takes to attract your date to you and create a great first impression.

Look Presentable for Your Date

Basic hygiene is a must. Think about it; would you like to go on a date with someone who has body odor issues or someone who shows you what they had for dinner last night, just by smiling? Take care of your basic hygiene. This means that a hot shower is indicated. Brush your teeth and wash your hair before your date. Make sure that you are clean, smell fresh and good and look presentable from the skin outward.

Remember, making yourself look and smell presentable is only the first step. You'll feel more confident when you look and smell clean, but you'll feel even better when you smell good. Use a mouthwash to rinse your mouth and don't forget the deodorant. Make sure that the deodorant isn't overwhelming though. It may seem like a lot of work right now – although, it really isn't – but you won't regret it when you get close to your date.

Dress Smartly and Appropriately

Make sure that what you wear isn't dowdy or ill-fitting. Find clothes that are striking and look good on your figure or enhance it. Also keep in mind where you're going for your date. After all, you don't want to dress up in smart but casual jeans for an evening at the opera. If you are planning to attend the opera, you'll need a proper suit or evening gown. Otherwise, based on the venue, you can go for a neatly pressed pair of khakis with a button down shirt or a cocktail dress or smart blouse and skirt. Whatever you wear should be at once stylish and comfortable. Remember, it isn't about just looking good but feeling good too.

If you're meeting up for a light lunch or even just coffee, don't bother getting all dressed up. As mentioned earlier, decide what you'll wear based upon where you're going. Color always brightens things up, so wearing something with it is always a good idea. Bright colors make you seem bold and vibrant, as per studies conducted.

Style and Groom

A clean up and a good outfit are absolutely necessary but looking presentable doesn't just stop there. Your general appearance also includes things such as hair, nails and in the case of men, beards and/or moustaches. Make sure that your hair looks neat and well-groomed. Gentlemen, keep your beard or moustache (if you have one) trimmed and neat, too. Cut your nails if necessary. Ladies, that would mean that a manicure and a pedicure is in order. Chipped nail polish is not attractive.

It's a first date, so it is safe to assume that your appearance will be examined quite closely. After all, you'll be doing the same with your date. Keep this assumption in mind while getting ready and you won't miss anything. A spray of a delicate perfume or understated cologne is a good idea, but don't empty half the bottle on yourself.

Smile

Be ready to smile a lot. It is natural to feel nervous and uncomfortable, but try not to let is show. Smile and act as naturally as possible. Smiling makes you seem attractive to your date. It also does wonders for your own mood.

Research shows that when you smile you radiate positivity and others feel as though they can trust you. Of course, it also lets people know that you're a fun person. As mentioned above, smiling also helps ease your own nerves when you start feeling edgy and, perhaps, just a bit jittery before the date or while on the date.

Plan an Interesting Date

A first date can be nerve-wracking enough without having to sit and think of things to talk about to keep the conversation going. Most people go out for dinner or a movie or both on a first date, but if you feel that that is too intimidating or too much pressure, you have other options. You can try a new bar, go for a long walk, get tickets to a concert or show or game that both of you enjoy or even enjoy a quiet picnic. You can even attend a cooking class for couples if that is what interests you.

It's not uncommon to feel a lot of pressure on a first date; after all, you're expected to make interesting conversation for hours with someone who is, for all intents and purposes, a perfect stranger. When you do something that doesn't just involve talking but doing things together, both of you can relax. You'll find that conversation is much smoother and an unusual activity makes for a date that both of you will remember for the right reasons.

Punctuality is a Must

If you've fixed seven as the time for your date, don't show up at seven-thirty. If you've committed to a time for the date, stick to it. It is also a good idea to check with your date if he or she is going to meet you at a pre-arranged location or whether you will pick them up or be picked up by them. Don't cut things too fine in terms of time. Make sure that you've taken care of any last minute details before you set out.

Try to arrive a little bit early for the date. Don't be too early, though. You don't want to seem desperate. Arriving five to ten minutes early shows that you are serious about the date. If the venue is new to you or if you are nervous or both, you can use this time to acquaint yourself with your surroundings and mentally

Politeness is Key

Being friendly is great, but something that can make your first date easier and more comfortable is good manners. Consideration always earns good marks. If the lady is ok with it, the gentleman should observe small courtesies such as picking up the check, opening doors and pulling out chairs. Ladies can also show some consideration by offering to go halves on the bill. Good manners put the other person at ease and help you avoid situations that could make them and you uncomfortable.

Don't do anything blindly. Be aware of your date's reactions to small gestures to see whether they receive them favorably or not. Not all ladies appreciate having doors opened for them and not all gentleman appreciate going halves on the bill. Don't force it if they don't want it. Consideration extends to not forcing good manners down their throats.

Don't ask clichéd questions

Nervousness about getting to know someone new can affect conversations. It is not uncommon that conversation during a first date begins to sound like an interview for a job. Asking your date about their hobbies, work and personal beliefs is fine but don't just stop there. Topics such as family, friends, favorite movies, books or music, enjoyable vacations and pets are all good ways to learn more about your date and to keep the conversation going. Try asking something unusual such as what they would do if they found out the world was going to end in a few days.

This is not a police interrogation either. Be tactful when you ask them about their preferences. Past relationships are a big no-no; frankly, it's none of your business. Work stresses are only to be talked about if they show an interest in talking about such a topic.

Show that You're Interested in Them

Give all your attention to your date. Show that you are genuinely interested in who they are and what they're saying. Eye contact and verbal confirmations such as 'uh-huh', 'yes' and 'I agree' are good ways to let them know that you are listening to them.

One of the biggest complaints that people have about a first date is that their date ends up taking over the conversation. If you find this trait annoying, you definitely don't want to emulate it. Conversing with someone is very different from being the only one doing the talking. Pay attention while they are talking and put in your two cents worth when the conversation is directed towards you. Gauge your date's mood throughout the conversation and be mindful of things such as whether they're comfortable and whether you may be talking too much.

Having a Good Time is Most Important

While going on a first date can be quite stressful, don't treat it as an obligation. Remember that under all that nervousness, you have asked for or agreed to the date, so you must be anticipating a good time too. Focus on that instead of the butterflies in your stomach. Try to have as much fun as possible and maintain a positive attitude. Entertain your date so that both you and he or she keep laughing. While you do want to make a good impression, don't start taking the date so seriously that you lose any sense of humor. It's inevitable that a part of your brain will try to keep analyzing the date while it is happening, but try to shut it off or at least don't listen to it. Relax and enjoy your date's company. After all, that is why you are here.

Make sure that your expectations of the date aren't sky high and that your motives are exactly what they should be – getting to know your date. Anything else and the date could become uncomfortable. Enjoy getting to know them and spending time with them.

Sometimes, if it feels as though the date isn't going as well as you thought, don't be afraid to change the situation a bit. For example, if your date looks bored at the opera, ask them if they would like to leave and suggest a few drinks at a fancy bar instead. Merely changing the environment can go a long way in making things less stressful and helping you enjoy each other's company.

Find Common Ground

In your conversation with your date, try to find out what both of you have in common and work on that. For example, if both of you enjoy trying out different cuisines, you can ask them for their opinion of a restaurant both of you have been to. If you enjoy the same type of movies, discuss those movies in detail if you want. Finding out what you have in common and working on it goes a long way in helping you connect more deeply with your date. Conversation also becomes much easier since you can talk about a lot of different things now.

Similarities are great but sometimes opposites work even better. If your date doesn't like something that you do, don't immediately decide that things won't work out. Sometimes their differing viewpoints will give you an insight into who they are and where they're coming from. You might find that an opposing opinion actually facilitates a better conversation than merely exploring similarities.

Ask for a Second Date

Once the evening is over and if the date has gone well, ask them if they would like to see you again. Let them know that you enjoyed spending time with them and had a good time. You can give them your phone number and ask them to text or call you. You can even ask for their phone number if you feel that they wouldn't mind giving it to you. A good first impression leaves the door open to you forming a connection that could end up being abiding.

Don't push it with the phone number – either yours or theirs. First, gauge how your date felt about your encounter. If your date has enjoyed it, asking for the phone number or offering your own is ok. Once you have the number, ensure that you call the other person or text them to tell them that you enjoyed yourself with them, within a couple of days.

Chapter 8

Develop Social Skills and Charisma

If you feel like you are always that one awkward guest at social events, or like you consistently struggle to get into new conversations because you are shy, then it is possible that this negative self-talk is affecting your career and social life. By improving your social skills, you will begin to feel more comfortable no matter the social situation, you will make new friends and have more fun when you go out—even when you are an introvert.

Start acting like a social person

This can be hard. You may find that instead of being out and talking to people all the time, you would rather head home instead. But over time, socializing will get easier.

This doesn't mean that you have to go and change your whole personality. There are so many great things about being an introvert, but if you can do a bit of acting and behave a little more social when you go out, even when you don't feel it, you may find that small talk and joining in on conversations can start to feel more natural. Don't allow anxiety or shyness to get in the way and make things more difficult. It is up to you to make the decision to talk to new people, and to start these conversations, even when you feel a bit nervous about it.

It is fine to start out small

As an introvert, you probably don't want to spend all your free time going to parties or putting yourself in a ton of social situations. Introverts can sometimes get nervous just seeing their calendar fill up for the month. They want to be able to sit back and enjoy some things, and sometimes after a long week at work, they would like to have a few nights off at home to be alone and to recharge before hitting the social scene again.

If going out each night to a party or spending a lot of time out in a crowd seems overwhelming to you, it is fine to start out small. You should still work your way up to being more social and going out at least occasionally. But a "slow and steady" approach can definitely get you there as well.

One way to start small, is to just say "Thank you" to the grocery store clerk the next time you go shopping. Then, after a few times of this, start making some small talk by mentioning the weather, or asking about the person's family, or how they are doing in school. This can help you get some more practice with small talk and can make it easier to engage in conversation with others when you do go out in more social settings.

It is easier to get others to talk about themselves

Many introverts find that it is uncomfortable to talk about themselves when they are with others. They feel that doing this makes them seem like they are bragging or puts the spotlight on them. They would much rather let the other person do most of the talking, and let the other person talk about themselves, while they spend the time asking lots of questions.

The good news is that you can easily turn the conversation around. In fact, you will find that many of the other people that you meet are going to really love talking about themselves. When they find an ear that is ready to listen, they will often just go on and on, and soon you will have made a good ally, and all you needed to do was ask questions and show your interest in that other person.

How do you get this all started? Simply ask a question about the other person. This can be about their family, about their hobbies, or about their career. Just keep asking questions, interjecting with some of your own information when asked, and otherwise just let the other person keep going. Encourage others to talk so that you won't have to be the one who is making all the idle chit-chat all the time.

To help with this, make sure that you are asking open-ended questions, which require more than a yes or a no answer from the other person. If you simply ask closed-ended questions, then you will get very short answers and most likely run out of conversation really quickly.

Also, if the other person does ask you some questions, try to give a full answer. Don't respond with only a "Yes" or "No", even if the question is a little bit closed ended. Doing this will shut down the effort that the other person has made, and they may feel like you don't want to keep the conversation going. Instead, choose to expand on any question that they ask, allowing both you and the other person to feed off each other.

Create goals for yourself

There are many different goals that you can set yourself in order to get the most out of your social improvement. You can choose to open your front door when someone rings the bell and talk with them for a few minutes. You can agree to sign up for a class or a workshop, and then make it your aim to talk to someone at each class. You can start attending a social activity in the community and go to regular meetings, where you will get to know other locals.

When you pick out goals, you must go with ones that will challenge you a bit, that will push you out of your comfort zone, but which won't be so difficult that you aren't able to reach them. Establish a goal and then pick out the right strategies that will help you to attain it, so you end up improving your social life, step-by-step.

Start out with one goal at a time when you are doing this, so that you don't take on too much at once. Pick one of the goals above, or a different social goal that appeals to you, and then build up from there. This way, you can work off the success that you see from achieving the first goal, and build confidence and momentum to attempt the second goal, and so on.

Remember to compliment others

Compliments are going to be your best friend. They don't take long to come up with, and they will make the other person feel amazing. It is such a simple way to get on the good side of another person, and you will find that the conversation will flow much more freely as a result.

Compliments are one of the best ways for you to open the door to a new conversation. You can offer one of your co-workers a compliment on how hard they worked on the presentation they just gave. You can compliment a friend on their new promotion, or a neighbor for getting a new car. There is always something that you can praise another person for, even if it is as simple as pointing out that you like their jacket, and asking where they got it from.

Compliments should show others that you are friendly. Friendly people are willing to give out compliments, whether they know the person well or not, and leading the discussion with a compliment, or finding another natural place to add it in, can go a long way.

Try it the next time that you meet someone new. Take a few seconds while you are being introduced to find something about that person that you can praise them on. You can choose their outfit, their shoes, their handshake, their hair, or something else. The compliment doesn't have to be big, but it shows that you are really noticing the other person and helps draw them to you.

Keep yourself up to date on any current events

One of the hardest things that you have to deal with when working on small talk, is finding topics to discuss with other people. There are many different topics you can discuss with another person, including friends, family, hobbies, career, interests, and current events.

Current events, as long as they are not too controversial, can be a great topic to bring up, and can lead to a longer conversation as you and the other person go back and forth on the different stories in the news that you have read about. The best way to take advantage of this is to keep up to date on all the news stories and current trends that you can find, which will help you to have something to talk about on any occasion. For example, you can look online, watch the news, and read magazines to help you out.

The important thing is to avoid any topic that is too controversial, including religion and politics. You don't want to ruin a potential friendship just because you decided to bring up politics in the first few minutes of meeting someone new. But do take the time to talk about any of the other current events and news stories that may be of interest.

Practice makes perfect

Practice is one of the best ways to help you improve your social skills. If you just read through this guidebook, but never get out in a social situation to use these suggestions, then they are just theories and you will never get better. You have to put yourself in social situations to help you get in some practice to see the progress that you want to make.

Anyone, including a shy introvert, can learn how to improve their social skills. It can take time, and you may make mistakes along the way, but it is going to be so worth it in the long run. The more that you can get out and the longer you practice, the better you will get at this endeavor.

Try getting out just a few times a month, and build up from there

For an introvert, it can sometimes be difficult to get yourself out there and into social situations. Sometimes just going to work and to the store throughout the week is enough to exhaust you. But if you want to work on your social skills, you need to avoid making excuses, and put yourself in social situations.

Likewise, if you are shy, you can also struggle to get out and meet people, but this is because you don't know how to express yourself and are afraid of being embarrassed or rejected. To gain confidence and get around this fear, while learning to communicate effectively, it is also important to get out and expose yourself more socially.

You don't have to go out every night of the week. You just need to get out a little more than usual. Even just adding one or two social events to your calendar a month can make a big difference in how much you work on your social skills. And the more you get out there, the more comfortable you will feel. In fact, you may even find that social activities, when limited and on your own terms, can be more enjoyable.

You get the freedom to pick out what social events you would like to attend, like a reading club at the library, or out with a few friends to get coffee. You can go to a meeting in the civic center of your town or just go out to a restaurant with your partner, instead of getting food delivered to your home. This all helps you to get out of the house, talk to different people, and to expand your comfort zone a little bit. The rest of the nights of the month can be reserved for going home and recharging at your own pace.

Identify and then replace any of the negative thoughts that you have

Many people who struggle with small talk and social interactions may also have a lot of negative thoughts about themselves as a result of this. This is particularly true if the person has difficulty because of intense shyness or social anxiety, and they may assume that no one likes them, that they are going to say something "stupid", or that they will just end up embarrassing themselves. The biggest problem with constantly entertaining these ideas is that they can become a self-fulfilling prophecy.

For example, it is harmful to tell yourself: "I'm so awkward, if I go to the party, no one will want to talk to me or I will just end up embarrassing myself." Because of these negative thoughts and the desire to avoid being embarrassed, you may just sit in the corner alone for the whole party. Then, when you leave, you will think that it must be true that you are too awkward, because no one talked to you all night.

If you want to get better at your social skills and learn how to communicate well with others, you need to learn how to get rid of these unhealthy thinking patterns. Start by identifying the negative thoughts that are dragging you down. Once you have found those, you can work on replacing them with other more positive and realistic thoughts, which will help to build your confidence instead.

By making these changes, you get to control your own destiny. Instead of thinking that you are awkward and certain to make mistakes, you can start out with a little pep talk to get through each social situation. For example, the next time that you go out to a social event, start out by telling yourself "I can make friendly conversation and I can meet new people."

It is so important that you don't allow yourself to dwell on unproductive thoughts that work against you and the change you want to inspire in your life. If a thought makes you feel bad about yourself, or keeps you from socializing with others, then it is destructive and should be challenged.

Having a good set of social skills is so essential when it comes to being an effective communicator. Great social skills are not easy, and everyone experiences awkwardness sometimes. You have to keep trying and keep putting yourself out there, even if you do happen to fail. You will get better over time, and these social skills can serve you well for your whole life. It's never too late to start trying some of these suggestions to help you change the way you see yourself, as you learn to communicate with ease.

Chapter 9

How to Keep a Conversation Alive

Initiating small talks to break an awkward silence or get to know someone can be a bit stressful, especially if you're not that knowledgeable about how to get it done. If you're still a beginner in small talks, and you plan to brush up your skills in this area, then probably among the first things that you have to research about are possible small talk starters. This chapter will cover some of the best topics that you can use to initiate small talks then turn them into smart conversations. You'll also gain some tips on how to be successful in using them.

Foods

Most of the situations that are suitable for initiating small talks involve food. This means that it's worthy to make this a subject when trying to open up a dialogue. For instance, you can talk about how the foods served in a party look amazing, and ask the other party which one he can recommend. You can also comment on the nice look of the food he's eating then follow it up with where he bought it.

You may also open up conversations by commenting on foods then asking about how they're prepared or the possible ingredients. Food is something that most people have in common, so if you open up a small talk using this topic, you'll most likely end up getting a response.

Compliments

It does not hurt to pay someone a compliment sometimes. In fact, it's an efficient way to start a conversation. Don't be too shy to let someone know if there is something about him/her that impresses you. For instance, you can comment on her beautiful brooch, then follow it up with a question about where he got it. You can also praise his fashion sense.

Compliments are not only limited to just the physical look. Note that you can also compliment him/her about his skills, such as his ability to write a very nice story or opinion on a certain matter. You can also let him know how you admire his ability to take on a lot of responsibilities in a calm manner. This kind of topic builds a strong connection considering the fact that it mainly focuses on positivity. You're telling someone something good about himself/herself, which can instantly help you connect and earn his/her interest.

Interests

You may also initiate a small talk by talking about the possible interests that you have in common. For instance, if you're in a place where film buffs are around, you can ask someone beside you if he's also in the film industry or if he's a movie addict just like you. This will give the both of you something to talk about.

If you're talking to a teacher, then you can tell him/her about how impressed you are with his work. You can then follow it up with what makes him love teaching and other perks of being an educator. By tapping into someone's interest and showing him that you're also interested on it, you earn yourself a new acquaintance who's willing to talk to you about something.

Specific Location or Occasion you're in

If you want to break the ice when you are in a specific location or occasion, then comment on something about a specific situation. Observe and look around. Find out if there is something that is worthwhile to point out. Some examples would be telling someone beside you how nice the room or venue is, how incredible the foods and the services are, or how nicely decorated the entire venue is. If the person you're talking to also loves what you're seeing, then he'll most likely respond, giving the both of you something to talk about.

Pets

You may also ask someone about his pets. Pets are usually the most common grounds of people who can't seem to find something in common to talk about. If you are a pet lover, in general, then it will be easy for you to relate to others who love pets, as well. The good thing about this is that you can still expect to successfully initiate the small talk using this topic regardless of the specific animal he loves – be it dogs, cats, birds, horses, or the wildlife. While some may get annoyed if you talk about your own pet, note that asking them about theirs is an efficient technique in letting them open up and have fun.

Current Events

If you want to be a master of small talks, then it would also be nice to learn more about current events. Try to read newspapers or watch the news on TV so you'll get an idea about the recent events in society right now. This will instantly give you an idea about what to talk about. There's a great chance that those around you know about this, as well, so talking to them about it will instantly open up smart conversations.

Make sure that you're fully aware of what's happening in your city and the world. The good news is that you can now access important news information digitally. You can get them directly from reliable news sites or access them on social media. These digital sources can help keep you current, so you'll never run out of ideas when talking to someone.

Weather

While it's true that the weather seems a mundane topic to talk about, it's actually a neutral small talk starter, which everyone can easily discuss. For instance, if there was a recent storm, then you can talk about it. You can also comment about the nice weather and follow it up with a question about what he usually does in such a good weather.

Arts and entertainment

These cover topics like latest TV shows and movies, popular music and books or famous restaurants. Just make sure that you prepare for such topics, if you're planning to use it to initiate small talks next time. Familiarize yourself about what's hot in the arts and entertainment field. Reading books can also make you more informed in this area, making it easier for you to think of something that you can talk about.

Sports

These encompass topics like favorite teams, bowl games, tournaments and other sporting events. The good thing about this is that even if you're not a sports fan, there's still something to discuss. For instance, you can tell the person you're talking to about the specific reasons why you hate sports.

Another tip is to keep a record of specific sports played on specific seasons like golf, hockey, football and soccer. This will make it easier for you to think about the best small talk topics relevant to sports. If the Olympics is ongoing, for instance, then there's a great chance that everyone will talk about it when you open up a conversation.

Family

Some people will most likely talk to you by asking about your family. For instance, you may receive questions about whether you have brothers or sisters, how many are you in the family, whether you have children, how long are you and your spouse together, etc. Prepare yourself for these questions and topics as someone will most likely ask these to you during small talks. You can also reciprocate by raising questions about their family.

Work

Work is also another good topic for small talks. Ask about the current job of the person you're talking to and what he likes the most about it. Be willing to share information about your work, as well, as you'll most likely be asked the same.

Vacations / Travel Destinations

Another topic, which is worthy to discuss is travel or vacation. Most people love to go to places, so be prepared to talk about this If you want to initiate small talks. If you travel a lot, then be willing to share your opinions and experiences about your previous travel destinations to someone who's asking.

Make sure to ask them regarding their dream destination or favorite spot, as well. Also, try to ask for their recommendations. Most of them will be more than happy to recommend a nice place to you and share their knowledge about it. This is a good way to transition the small talk into more meaningful conversations.

Aside from the ones already mentioned, other topics that you can use to successfully initiate small talks then keep the conversation going are hobbies, hometown, and celebrity gossips. The good thing about these topics is that these are safe and low-risk, meaning they will most likely elicit a positive response.

There's a lower chance that you'll fail if you use the mentioned topics since most of them engage the people around you while letting you identify common grounds.

Conclusion

Now we come to the end where we put together everything we have learned. It is my hope that you feel more confident and aware of how to make small talk with people and how to use those skills to build lasting, fulfilling relationships. You should now know how to make an excellent first impression that creates lasting positive memories in those you talk to. You are also likely better at reading the body language and facial expressions of others, and hopefully, you can now adjust and manipulate your own to hide your fear and give off the confident and assertive vibes you are trying to project.

I also hope that you feel better able to handle fear and shame. Rejection and not being liked are concerns for all of us, but none of us like every single person we meet. If you remind yourself that even if things do not pan out between you and your new acquaintance, you ultimately did not lose anything by trying. In fact, your efforts will always reward you with valuable skills in talking to others you meet- many of which will reap the results you actually endeavored to achieve. You will not share like interests or qualities with everyone you meet and sometimes a conversation will wind up not going anywhere. That is okay! Do not get disheartened if you cannot befriend every single person you chat with. Not all of them will have personalities and passions that complement your own, after all. Rejection can hurt but not trying at all guarantees you fail, and a gentle rejection due to simple incompatibility can be better for everyone sometimes. Failing is not an excuse to stop trying, but if you follow the tips we discussed here, you are highly likely to succeed more often than not.

We also discussed ways to add depth and intimacy to your mundane conversations, eventually enabling you to turn them into genuine friendships. This is done by listening to what your chat partner is saying, asking for more details, and bonding over shared interests or experiences. Even when one of their interests is something you are largely unfamiliar with, admitting that and asking for more information will grant you a relatively pleasant conversational topic. People enjoy talking about themselves, and your acquaintances will appreciate your listening skills if you can carry on even a conversation that is more focused on them. As time goes on, you will discover more things that you share and will become more comfortable together. Eventually, you will find yourself exchanging contact information and getting together to chat and do things together more frequently, building the foundations of a beautiful friendship.